9 99
Snld BK

HIGHLIGHTS OF NASCAR RACING™

THE BIGGEST NASCAR RACES

HOLLY CEFREY

rosen publishing's
rosen central®

New York

To my family

Published in 2008 by The Rosen Publishing Group, Inc.
29 East 21st Street, New York, NY 10010

Library of Congress Cataloging-in-Publication Data

Cefrey, Holly.
The biggest NASCAR races / Holly Cefrey. — 1st ed.
    p. cm. — (Highlights of NASCAR racing)
Includes bibliographical references.
ISBN-13: 978-1-4042-1399-9 (library binding)
1. Stock car racing—United States. 2. NASCAR (Association) I. Title.
GV1029.9.S74C383 2008
796.72—dc22

2007035825

Manufactured in the United States of America

On the cover: Jack Sprague, Johnny Benson, and Travis Kvapil lead the field to the finish line at Daytona International Speedway on February 16, 2007.

CONTENTS

NASCAR racing is an extreme sport. Pictured here are the racers of the Nextel Cup Series. Racers compete all season long to be the champion. Winners earn a place in racing history.

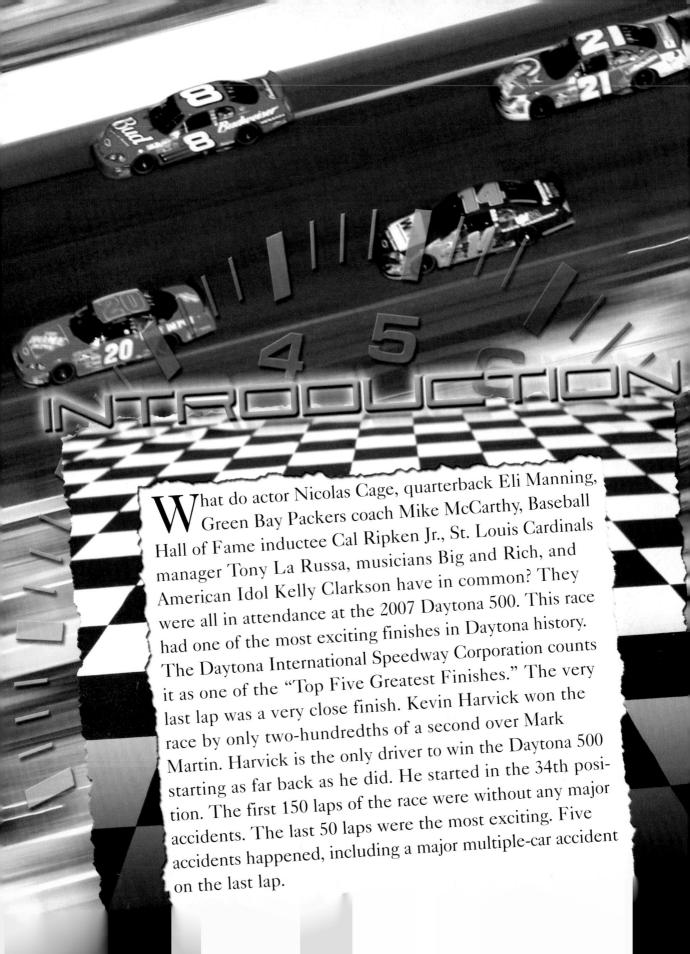

INTRODUCTION

What do actor Nicolas Cage, quarterback Eli Manning, Green Bay Packers coach Mike McCarthy, Baseball Hall of Fame inductee Cal Ripken Jr., St. Louis Cardinals manager Tony La Russa, musicians Big and Rich, and American Idol Kelly Clarkson have in common? They were all in attendance at the 2007 Daytona 500. This race had one of the most exciting finishes in Daytona history. The Daytona International Speedway Corporation counts it as one of the "Top Five Greatest Finishes." The very last lap was a very close finish. Kevin Harvick won the race by only two-hundredths of a second over Mark Martin. Harvick is the only driver to win the Daytona 500 starting as far back as he did. He started in the 34th position. The first 150 laps of the race were without any major accidents. The last 50 laps were the most exciting. Five accidents happened, including a major multiple-car accident on the last lap.

In turn four, Kyle Busch's car began to skid out of control, causing other drivers to crash. Racer David Stremme told the *Orlando Sentinel*, "All of a sudden, people were coming from everywhere, going places they shouldn't be going and driving like they shouldn't be driving. It was crazy." "Crazy" could describe Clint Bowyer's finish. His car crossed the finish line upside down and on fire. It then flipped right-side up and he escaped without harm. Other drivers involved in the last-lap accident were Matt Kenseth, Jeff Gordon, David Gilliland, Casey Mears, Sterling Marlin, Greg Biffle, and Elliott Sadler.

The Daytona 500 has become known as the "Great American Race." It has the biggest payout, or prize money, of any auto sport. The 2007 payouts were more than $18 million. Racer Kevin Harvick received more than $1.5 million for winning.

The Daytona 500 occurs every year in Daytona Beach, Florida. This is also where NASCAR began—NASCAR stands for the National Association for Stock Car Auto Racing. Stock-car racing uses cars that have standard auto bodies. They are not specially designed for racing. Rather, they are cars that come from commercial "stock" designs— "commercial" means publicly available. Commercial car companies that have had their stock cars raced in NASCAR events include Chevrolet, Ford, and Dodge.

NASCAR is the official organization that makes the rules for stock-car racing in the United States. It has authority over all of the drivers and teams that race in NASCAR events. If they do not follow the rules, NASCAR can give them penalties such as fines. NASCAR also makes sure that racetracks are run properly and safely.

NASCAR is a globally recognized organization with very humble beginnings. "Big Bill" France Sr. (William Henry Getty France) started the organization. Big Bill moved to Daytona Beach from Washington,

Daytona 500 winners are given a copy of the Harley J. Earl Trophy. The original trophy stays at the track and has the name of every Daytona 500 winner on it.

D.C., in 1934. When he moved to Daytona Beach, a racing culture already existed there. Drivers from all over came to race on the beach. They used the hard-packed sand surface as a speedway.

Soon, the city organized races in order to bring in tourism money. Big Bill owned a service station and mechanic shop. Many racers thought of his shop as a hub, or center. He was a respected mechanic and racer in the racing culture. In 1938, the city asked him to organize the next big race.

Big Bill's first race was a success. He recruited, or attracted, skilled drivers and asked local businesses to give prizes. He sold tickets for 50 cents. More than 4,000 people came to watch. Big Bill saw that the sport had great appeal, or likability. He also knew that drivers and teams needed rules to follow and respect. With respected rules and a ruling organization, the sport would be respected, too.

In 1947, Big Bill and his friends organized the National Championship Stock Car Circuit, or NCSCC. The NCSCC would be responsible for setting up a point system and prizes. A point system keeps track of wins within a racing season. A racer with the most points at the end of the season would win the prize or purse. This would keep racers coming back to each event. The success of NCSCC would depend on whether racetracks and racers would accept it. Big Bill held a meeting with track leaders and racers. They eagerly discussed NCSCC's plans. His organization officially became NASCAR in 1948.

In 1949, NASCAR introduced a racing division known as "Strictly Stock." By 1959, Big Bill had cleared the way for a new super race-track: Daytona International Speedway. That same year, the first Daytona 500 was held. More than 40,000 people attended. Lee Petty won the race. Lee Petty was the father of famous racer Richard Petty. There are two more generations of Pettys who raced: Richard's son and grandson. Unfortunately, Petty's grandson Adam died in a prac-tice race accident in 2000.

A family of racers is known as a racing dynasty. There are seven-teen racing dynasties. NASCAR is a family dynasty as well. Big Bill retired in 1972 and his son, Bill Jr., became president. NASCAR is now run by Brian France, Big Bill's grandson. Other family members, such as Bill France Jr.'s wife and daughter, have served in important positions within the organization.

In addition to the Strictly Stock division, NASCAR has two other divisions: Modified and Roadsters. ("Modified" means changed from its original form.) The Strictly Stock division has had a few name changes since it began. It was known as the Grand National Series, then the Winston Cup, and it is now the Nextel Cup. In 2008, because Nextel and Sprint have merged, it will be called the Sprint Cup.

NASCAR has two other major national series. They are the Busch Series and the Craftsman Truck Series. NASCAR also oversees eight regional series and one local series. It is the authority over 1,500 races at more than 100 tracks in the United States, Canada, and Mexico. Let's take a look at the series of NASCAR!

CHAPTER ONE

The Nextel Cup Series

You may wonder how racing series get their names. Series like Nextel Cup are named after sponsors. Sponsors are individuals or organizations that support another person, organization, or activity by giving money to it. Companies become sponsors of NASCAR because doing so will help them reach a very large fan base.

According to NASCAR, its events are broadcast in more than 150 countries to 75 million fans. This means that a sponsor advertisement is seen by millions of people who may become instant buyers. Even a small percent of the 75 million buyers can greatly boost a company's sales. Sponsors have advertisements for the events. If they sponsor a race team, the car will use its colors and/or logo. The driver will promote its products. Walls of the track also have sponsor signs.

NASCAR benefits from having sponsors. It can create new fans from the sponsors' loyal buyers. It also uses sponsor funds to maintain and improve tracks. Funds are put into a series purse, making it more exciting for racers and fans.

In the world of racing, drivers are great spokespersons. Racers are heroes to many people. Here Bill Elliot rushes out to greet fans in 2003.

Nextel/Sprint Joins NASCAR

Nextel decided to sponsor the Winston Cup Series in 2003. R. J. Reynolds was the previous sponsor. The company makes Winston cigarettes, among other products. R. J. Reynolds was the first company to sponsor a whole series, so the name was changed from the Grand National Cup to the Winston Cup. Sponsorship began in 1971, when R. J. Reynolds promoted the series and funded drivers and teams. This sponsorship became controversial, or troubled. The dangerous effects of cigarette smoking became widely known. The cigarette sponsorship began to seem inappropriate.

Nextel became the next sponsor of the Winston Cup in 2004. According to NASCAR, Nextel will spend $700 million over a ten-year period to support the series. Officials of both companies saw this as a great idea. The chief executive officer of Nextel, Tim Donahue, told NASCAR, "Both of our organizations began as upstarts . . . not a lot of people took us seriously. But look at us now: America's number-one spectator sport and America's most successful wireless company joining forces."

From the Beginning

The Nextel Cup got its start all the way back in 1949. It was known as the Strictly Stock division. Drivers used late-model family sedans.

Teams were allowed to tweak, or improve, the engine, but they were not allowed to change anything else about the car. It was raced as it came, straight from the manufacturer.

According to NASCAR, the first race included a wide variety of car makes. The cars were Buick, Cadillac, Chrysler, Ford Hudson, Kaiser, Lincoln, Mercury, and Oldsmobile. Many early racers would drive their cars to the track to race them, as they were little different from when they were commercially bought.

Tracks of the 1950s put these cars to the test. Many cars experienced failures or strain due to the track conditions and heavy racing. Tires made especially for racing—to last longer than regular tires—were created in the early 1950s. Otherwise, street tires would blow due to heat and wear of the track. Oldsmobile, Lincoln, and Hudson introduced severe usage kits. The kits allowed for stronger axles, hubs, and spindles. These are

The Tracks of the Nextel Cup Series

SH = under 1 mile (1.6 kilometers) long
INT = less than 2 miles (3.2 km), but greater than 1 mile
SS = longer than 2 miles
RC = a road course with twists and turns

Atlanta Motor Speedway—INT
Bristol Motor Speedway—SH
California Speedway—SS
Chicagoland Speedway—INT
Darlington Raceway—INT
Daytona International Speedway—SS
Dover International Speedway—SH
Homestead-Miami Speedway—INT
Indianapolis Motor Speedway—SS
Infineon Raceway—RC
Kansas Speedway—INT
Las Vegas Motor Speedway—INT

Lowe's Motor Speedway—INT
Martinsville Speedway—SH
Michigan International Speedway—SS
New Hampshire International Speedway—INT
Phoenix International Raceway—SH
Pocono Raceway—SS
Richmond International Raceway—SH
Talladega Superspeedway—SS
Texas Motor Speedway—INT
Watkins Glen International—RC

NASCAR races have changed since the 1950s. Many racetracks were dirt, and cars were driven straight from the street. Now, modified cars based on standard models are used.

part of the car's suspension. They are how the wheels connect to the chassis, or frame, of the car. Manufacturers were paying attention to the races because they learned how to make their products better.

The current cars of NASCAR are no longer what you would buy from your commercial carmakers. They need only a few original stock parts, such as the roof, hood and rear deck lid body parts, and engine block. The rest of the car is built for speed and racing. They can reach speeds greater than 200 miles (322 kilometers) per hour.

Familiar Friends

Many of racing's most famous names come from the Nextel Cup Series. Earnhardt, Petty, Elliot, Labonte, Waltrip, Yarborough, Gordon, and Jarrett are familiar names to anyone who has watched NASCAR racing. They arrive here from many years of racing, racing in the other divisions, or after a few years on local tracks. Some Nextel Cup racers join the series after racing other types of vehicles, such as karts.

These big names earn their fame. They have several races under their belts and numerous Nextel wins. Darrel Waltrip has 84 wins; 47 of these wins occurred on short tracks. Jeff Gordon has 70 wins, with 16 superspeedway wins and 15 short-track wins. Dale Earnhardt Sr. had 79 wins, with 29 superspeedway wins and 27 short-track wins. He died in 2001 in the Daytona 500.

Point System and the Chase

A driver, the owner, and the car manufacturer are awarded points for racing in the series. A driver who wins a NASCAR race wins 185 points. The runner-up wins 180 points. The number keeps getting lower,

depending on what finish the driver placed. If the driver placed 43rd or last place, he gets 34 points.

A driver can get extra points for how he raced during the event. If he led at least one lap, he gets five points. If he led the most laps, he gets five more points. For years, racers worked through the season, trying to earn points, but many were happy just placing within the top ten. That was until the Chase was introduced.

The Chase was added to the Nextel point system in 2004. Racers are awarded as above, but at the 26th race of each season, things change. The top 12 point leaders at the time of the 26th race are instantly qualified to enter the "Chase for the Championship."

At this time, every qualified driver will receive new points. Each receives 5,000. He also receives a ten-point bonus for every winning race within the first 26 races. This makes the racing in the start of the season more competitive as racers and teams strive to rack up the most wins. If the driver is not among the top 12 point leaders at the 26th race, he doesn't qualify for that year's championship.

CHAPTER TWO

The Busch Series

The Busch Series is considered a training ground for new racers who want to become Nextel Cup drivers. Oftentimes, Busch race events are scheduled at the same tracks and times as Nextel Cup events. Nextel racers take advantage of this by racing in the Busch Series. Since the races are on the same track, it gives Nextel Cup racers a feel for the track before the big race. This allows rookies, or new racers, to benefit from veteran racers' techniques. It also allows fans to get a peak at tomorrow's big-name racers.

The Busch Series is sponsored by Anheuser-Busch, a company that makes Busch beer and other products. The Busch Series got its start in 1950 under another name. It was called the Sportsman Division.

Names Change, Tracks Change, NASCAR Remains

The Sportsman Division was designed for avid, or dedicated, racers. The races took place on shorter tracks, with about 60 races per season. This meant that three or four races occurred per week. Several regional circuits took part in the series. By 1968, the division had a new name,

"Racin' the way it ought'a be" is the slogan for Bristol Speedway in Bristol, Tennessee. Up to 160,000 fans watch the excitement of NASCAR at the speedway.

the Late Model Sportsman Division. The cost of racing three to four times a week was increasing, so the 60 races per season were cut back to slightly more than 30. The events moved to longer tracks as well, like the Daytona International Speedway.

Anheuser-Busch decided to sponsor a series, and, in 1982, NASCAR pulled together all of the regions into a touring series. The combined series was called NASCAR Budweiser Late Model Sportsman Series. It was changed to the NASCAR Busch Grand National Series in 1998. Since 2003, it has been simply called the Busch Series.

After 2007, Anheuser-Busch no longer sponsored the series. This means that NASCAR needs to look for a new sponsor. You will be seeing the name change again, but to what is unknown. So far this

Pictured here is a wild crash scene at the original Daytona Speedway in the 1950s. It occurred during Speed Week.

year, possible companies include Kentucky Fried Chicken, Dunkin Donuts, Wal-Mart, and Subway. Anheuser-Busch funded about $10 million for the series each year. NASCAR hopes to get about $30 million a year with the new sponsor.

The Busch Cars

For the 2007 season, there are 35 races. Two of these races occur in Mexico and Canada. Eight of the races are exclusive Busch Series events. The rest are combination events with Nextel Cup and the Craftsman Truck Series. Combined events make it easier for Nextel Cup drivers to race in the Busch Series.

THE BIGGEST NASCAR RACES

The original cars of the series were past-edition commercial cars, or older models than what was then available. When the series started including long tracks, drivers began using larger Nextel Cup late models.

Today, cars of the Nextel and Busch Series look very similar, leading many people to ask, "What's the difference?" One difference is wheelbase. The wheelbase is the distance from the centerline of the front wheels to the centerline of the rear wheels. The wheelbase for Busch

The cars of all NASCAR series must conform or be made to very detailed specifications. Drivers need their cars to pass inspections so they can race and rack up points.

cars is 105 inches (2.66 meters). It is 110 inches (2.79 meters) for Nextel Cup cars. The shorter wheelbase allows for quicker turning, which is needed for short oval tracks. Other differences include speed and power, width and length, and weight. Nextel Cup cars are more powerful than Busch cars. This is a good thing when it comes to rookies. As you develop your driving skills, you can move into the class with more powerful cars. Having too much power before you're skilled can lead to deadly wrecks.

Winners and Big-Time Racers

Many big-name racers in Nextel have also rolled through the Busch Series. These racers include the 1998 and 1999 Busch champion Dale Earnhardt Jr., as well as the 1991 Busch champion Bobby Labonte. The winner of the 2007 Daytona 500, Kevin Harvick, was the Busch champion in 2006.

The Tracks of the Busch Series

SH = under 1 mile (1.6 km) long
INT = less than 2 miles (3.2 km), but greater than 1 mile
SS = longer than 2 miles
RC = a road course with twists and turns

Atlanta Motor Speedway—INT
Autodromo Hermanos Rodriguez—RC
Bristol Motor Speedway—SH
Chicagoland Speedway—INT
California Speedway—SS
Circuit Gilles Villeneuve—RC
Darlington Raceway—INT
Daytona International Speedway—SS
Dover International Speedway—SH
Gateway International Raceway—INT
Homestead-Miami Speedway—INT
Kansas Speedway—INT
Kentucky Speedway—INT

Lowe's Motor Speedway—INT
Memphis Motorsports Park—SH
Michigan International Speedway—SS
The Milwaukee Mile—SH
Nashville Superspeedway—INT
New Hampshire International Speedway—INT
O'Reilly Raceway Park—SH
Phoenix International Raceway—SH
Richmond International Raceway—SH
Talladega Superspeedway—SS
Texas Motor Speedway—INT
Watkins Glen International—RC

Pictured here is Dale Earnhardt Jr. He was the championship winner of the Busch Series for two years in a row. He won in 1998 and 1999.

There is controversy surrounding the Busch Series, however. When Nextel Cup drivers race in the Busch Series, they have an advantage over Busch-only racers. Nextel racers have big sponsorships and top-notch cars. They have experienced pit crews and the latest technology. According to *Sports Illustrated*, the top-five finishers in the 2006 Busch Series were Nextel Cup pros. Sixth place went to a Busch-only racer named Paul Menard. Even though he was in sixth place, he was more than 1,500 points behind the Nextel veteran winners in his division. Some drivers and fans think that Nextel professionals should not be allowed to race in the Busch Series.

This situation may change greatly over the next few years. NASCAR is developing "the Car of the Tomorrow" for the Busch class, and it will have a different chassis from the Nextel car. This will make Nextel teams reconsider racing in the Busch Series. The new Busch car will handle differently than

The Great American Race

The Daytona 500 is a race that many industry leaders, politicians, and celebrities love to attend. A lucky few are chosen to serve as grand marshals and honorary starters. Some musical artists are also invited to sing the national anthem.

Grand marshals yell, "Drivers, start your engines!"
1972: James Garner, actor
1975: Alejandro Orfila, ambassador of Argentina
1978: George H. W. Bush, CIA director
1980: August A. Busch III, great grandson of Anheuser-Busch founder
1999: Justice Clarence Thomas, Supreme Court associate
2003: John Travolta, actor
2006: James Caan, actor

1987: Jon Mills, Speaker of the House
1990: Anthony J. Celebrezze, Ohio attorney general
1993: Richard Petty, NASCAR legend
1999: Brett Favre, NFL quarterback
2000: Jackie Joyner-Kersee, Olympian
2004: Whoopi Goldberg, comedian/actor

National Anthem vocalists start the race off patriotically
1996: Engelbert Humperdinck
1998: Kathy Mattea
2001: O-Town
2002: Denise Graves
2004: LeAnn Rimes
2006: Fergie

Honorary starters wave the green flag to start the 200-lap race
1979: Ben Gazarra, actor
1983: George H. W. Bush, vice president of the United States

the Nextel car. Therefore, practicing on the track during the Busch Series won't help a Nextel driver get the true feel of the track.

Scoring

The Busch Series does not have a Chase for the Championship system like the Nextel Cup. Instead, the standard NASCAR scoring system is used. The driver with the most points at the end of the season is

The 2006 Busch Series champion Kevin Harvick joyously holds the series trophy. Drivers, crew members, and car owners get to share in the spotlight.

awarded the Busch Championship. A driver who wins a race gets 185 points. The runner-up gets 180 points. The number keeps getting lower, depending on what finish the driver placed. If the driver placed 43rd or last place, he gets 34 points.

The driver can get extra points for how he raced during the event. If he led at least one lap, he gets five points. If he led the most laps, he gets five more points. The most points a driver can earn at the finish of each race are 195. This system causes drivers to race consistently, or evenly, over a season.

CHAPTER THREE

The Craftsman Truck Series

The Craftsman Truck Series is the newest major national series for NASCAR. The first race was held on February 5, 1995. It was certainly something new to NASCAR: racing trucks instead of cars. The trucks are based on half-ton, short-bed, pickup-truck models. "Short bed" means the back part of the truck (payload) is shorter than the average bed. The trucks were first shown to the public in 1994. Brian France was a driving force behind making it a new series.

The series is sponsored by Craftsman Tools. The Sears and Roebuck Company owns Craftsman. The Craftsman brand has been a natural fit as a sponsor for NASCAR. According to the Auto Channel, 90 percent of homes in the United States have at least one Craftsman tool. It is a trusted and recognizable brand. The Craftsman Truck Series was originally called the SuperTruck Series. Craftsman Tools saw the appeal of the SuperTruck Series, and it immediately decided to become a sponsor. The racing series began in regional areas on short tracks. With Craftsman sponsorship, it quickly blossomed into a national sport, including long tracks like

The Craftsman brand goes hand-in-hand with the truck series of NASCAR. Craftsman Tools are marketed as tough and ever-lasting. The trucks of the Craftsman Truck Series are super tough, too.

Daytona International Speedway. Currently, there are 25 races per season in 19 U.S. states.

American Made

Since joining the series, Toyota has done very well. In 2006, it won the manufacturer's championship of the series. Todd Bodine, driving a Toyota Tundra, took the 2006 series championship as well. The top six finishers in the 2006 season were Tundra drivers. While traditional Ford and Chevrolet teams may not have liked the addition of Toyota, it has quickly become part of the NASCAR family.

Todd Bodine is the 2006 champion of the Craftsman Truck Series. Winning the championship is a lifelong dream for many racers. Bodine's brothers are also well-known racers.

Bill France Jr. was not against using non-American manufacturers. He approved so long as the cars were made in America. This meant jobs for Americans and a boost for the economy. The other three manufacturers for the Craftsman Series are Ford, Chevrolet, and Dodge. A German company now owns Dodge, but the models are still made in America.

Big Names Coming and Going

Like the Busch Series, the Craftsman Truck Series is a good starting point for rookie drivers. Kevin Harvick, Greg Biffle, Carl Edwards, Scott Riggs, and Kurt Busch have launched into Nextel after driving in the series. Edwards told the Auto Channel, "It provides a great opportunity for young drivers to get their start. I don't know how I ever would have made it to the Busch or Nextel Cup level without the Craftsman Truck Series."

The series is also a great place for Nextel and seasoned drivers to continue their racing careers. Bobby (Charles) Hamilton, Ted Musgrave, Johnny Benson, Jimmy Spencer, Ricky Craven, and Ron Hornaday Jr. have enjoyed dipping into the Craftsman Truck Series from Nextel. The top three all-time winners in the series are Ron Hornaday Jr. (32 wins), Jack Sprague (28 wins), and Mike Skinner (23 wins).

This environment, where veterans and rookies mix, can make for exciting racing. Rookies strive to outrun their heroes, while Nextel legends have fun with a new type of auto. The trucks provide different handling than Nextel or Busch cars.

Tough Stuff

The Craftsman Truck Series has a reputation for being tough. Because the trucks are hearty, powerful vehicles, the racing style is action-packed. Fans have come to rely on the fender-to-fender racing style of the series. Points for leaders have been so close each season that even the season's last race is a neck-and-neck battle for the champi-onship. One

The Tracks of the Craftsman Truck Series

SH = under 1 mile (1.6 km) long
INT = less than 2 miles (3.2 km), but greater than 1 mile
SS = longer than 2 miles
RC = a road course with twists and turns

Atlanta Motor Speedway—INT
Bristol Motor Speedway—SH
California Speedway—SS
Daytona International Speedway—SS
Dover International Speedway—SH
Gateway International Raceway—INT
Homestead-Miami Speedway—INT
Kansas Speedway—INT
Kentucky Speedway—INT
Las Vegas Motor Speedway—INT
Lowe's Motor Speedway—INT

Mansfield Motorsports Speedway—SH
Martinsville Speedway—SH
Memphis Motorsports Park—SH
Michigan International Speedway—SS
The Milwaukee Mile—SH
Nashville Superspeedway—INT
New Hampshire International Speedway—INT
O'Reilly Raceway Park—SH
Phoenix International Raceway—SH
Talladega Superspeedway—SS
Texas Motor Speedway—INT

Craftsman Truck Series past and present champions: (left to right) Mike Skinner, Jack Sprague, Ron Hornaday, Greg Biffle, Travis Kvapil, Mike Bliss, and Bobby Hamilton.

such example was the 2003 season, when four drivers had a chance to claim the championship in the final race. They were Brendan Gaughan, Travis Kvapil, Ted Musgrave, and Dennis Setzer. Kvapil won. Many of the finishes in the races are extremely close. At the finish line, the winner and runner-up are commonly separated by less than a second.

Scoring

The Craftsman Truck Series does not have a Chase for the Championship system like the Nextel Cup. Instead, the standard NASCAR scoring system is used. The driver with the most points at the end of the season is awarded the Craftsman Truck Championship. A driver who wins a race wins 185 points. The runner-up wins 180 points. The number keeps getting lower, depending on what finish the driver placed. If the driver placed 43rd or last place, he gets 34 points.

A driver can get extra points for how he raced during the event. If he led at least one lap, he gets five points. If he led the most laps, he gets five more points. The most points a driver can earn at the finish of each race are 195.

CHAPTER FOUR

International Series

NASCAR seeks to allow global fans to root for their own local racing heroes within new NASCAR series. These include two exciting series north and south of America's borders. NASCAR has developed the Canadian Tire Series and the Mexico Series. NASCAR sponsors such as Nextel and Domino's Pizza have shown interest in supporting international series.

NASCAR's Mexican Base

In 2004, NASCAR announced the formation of NASCAR Mexico. It is the base of operations for stock-car racing in Mexico. NASCAR partners with a Mexican entertainment company called OCESA. The goal is that NASCAR racing, wherever it is done, will be televised and watched by a diverse, or varied, audience. Part of this goal is met by taking the American NASCAR series on the road. The Busch Series has raced in Mexico as part of its season. American racers, crews, and die-hard fans travel to Mexico for scheduled races. This brings money into the local economy. It also shows racers and fans that NASCAR is committed to supporting the sport locally.

The Mexican flag waves in the breeze in front of the new racers of NASCAR Mexico. More international drivers and fans will be a part of NASCAR's future.

Mexico Series

NASCAR formed the Desafio Corona Series, Mexico's first national stock-car series. NASCAR worked with OCESA to establish safety and rules. It updated existing racetracks and built new ones. The 2007 season has fourteen races scheduled over nine months. There are ten oval races and four road courses. Car models include the Pontiac Grand Prix, Dodge Stratus, and Ford Mustang. The Desafio Corona Series is now known as NASCAR Mexico Corona Series. In the U.S. press, it is simply called the Mexico Series.

The 2006 NASCAR Mexico Corona Series championship went to Rogelio Lopez. He is from Aguascalientes, Mexico. From this incredible

Rogelio Lopez was the first Mexican racer to win an oval race in the Busch East Series in 2007. He was the NASCAR Mexico Corona Series champion in 2006.

experience, he has joined the NASCAR Busch East Series. The Busch East Series is a regional series. Lopez will, like many racers, gain his skills while moving up the ranks. Other NASCAR Mexico racers who have joined the Busch Series are Jorge Goeters and Carolos Contreras.

As the Craftsman Truck Series and Busch Series serve as training grounds for the Nextel Cup, the Mexico Series will also have supporting series. In 2007, NASCAR launched the Mexico T4 Series. The car models include the Dodge Neon and Chevrolet Astra. Rookies can join this series in order to develop as drivers. They can then join the Mexico Corona Series as seasoned, competitive racers.

Canadian Tire Series

NASCAR opened a Canadian base, NASCAR Canada, in 2004. It partnered with the Sports Network, or TSN. TSN is an English-language sports media and broadcasting network. Unlike Mexico, Canada already has a strong stock-car culture. CASCAR, or the Canadian Association for Stock Car Auto Racing, has been the authority over local, regional, and national stock-car racing since 1981.

After creating a base in Canada, NASCAR created a partnership with CASCAR. The partnership did not last long, as CASCAR decided to sell itself to NASCAR. CASCAR became a part of NASCAR in 2006. That same year, NASCAR announced the creation of the

Canadian Tire Series. Canadian Tire will be the major long-term sponsor. It will feature 12 races, from May through September, with its first season in 2007. The series is replacing CASCAR's Super Series. The cars are similar to those of the Nextel Cup and Busch Series. Models include the Chevrolet Monte Carlo and the Pontiac Grand Prix. They have a wheelbase of 107.5 inches (273 centimeters). The series' current leaders are Andrew Ranger, Don Thomson Jr., and J. R. Fitzpatrick.

NASCAR's goal is to unite the world of racers and fans. Races are now held in Mexico and Canada. NASCAR is looking at other global locations as well.

So far, both international series have strong starts. Many championship drivers from other motorsports have joined the series. Once these series are running strong, NASCAR will focus on making international series in other parts of the world.

Drive for Diversity

A long-term goal of NASCAR is to open the sport of racing to women and minorities. NASCAR wants to have winners from all walks of life. Traditionally, most drivers have been white males. NASCAR is working with an organization called Access Marketing to make sure that women and all ethnic groups get the chance to be a part of NASCAR.

In 2004, the Drive for Diversity program was launched. Every year, it finds budding drivers and crewmembers within all motorsports who are women or are ethnically diverse. It helps these people develop so they have a real chance at joining NASCAR. Hundreds of drivers submit their resumes to the program. From that, a group is invited to participate in a testing and evaluation event. From that group, talented drivers will be developed so they can qualify as NASCAR drivers. Crewmembers also submit their resumes to qualify for an apprenticeship with a NASCAR team.

In 2007, the Drive for Diversity program developed seven drivers to participate in NASCAR series. Chris Bristol, Michael Gallegos, Jesus Hernandez, and Lloyd Mack joined the national series. Paul Harraka, Jessica Helberg, and Peter Hernandez joined the regional series.

In 2007, 12 people were chosen to join the Crew Member Development program. They were Gregory Eclarin, Joshua Hubbard, Colby Knotts, Gil Limon, Carl Mabon, Daniel Montecino, Desirae Olson, Donald Powell, Aimee Sexton, Johnnie Wade, Leuwell Wilson, and Amanda Zwierzycki. These individuals will attend "Pitcrew U," which is a training course. After attending, they are placed on an established NASCAR team, where they will have the chance at a possible life-long career.

A Safer NASCAR

The death of Dale Earnhardt Sr. in 2001 was a shocking moment in the sport. The crash happened fast but did not do great damage to the car. Earnhardt's car turned sideways and slammed into the outside wall. Many viewers could not believe that it caused the death of one of NASCAR's most experienced, legendary drivers.

Public outrage over Earnhardt's death forced NASCAR to work harder on its long-term safety plans. NASCAR has introduced the Car of Tomorrow, or COT. Both the Nextel Cup and Busch Series will have their own designs. The COT will allow for better safety, so that crashes like Earnhardt's won't result in death. The COT will be introduced over the next few years until it becomes the standard design in racing.

Feature	Benefit
Bigger cabin: 2.5 inches (6.4 centimeters) taller, 4 inches (10.2 cm) wider	More space around the driver for protection on impact
Seat position more centered	Driver is farther from side door in case of side impact
Double frame rail on driver's side	Provides support against side impact. Provides room for impact-absorbing materials
Side panels with impact materials	Shields driver in case of side impact
Redesigned fuel cell (holds gas) with thicker walls and padding	Reduces the risk of fires due to accidents or malfunctions
Adjustable rear wing	Replaces rear spoiler. Provides better balance and control
Front adjustable splitter	Allows easy modification for long or short tracks, creating better balance and control

CHAPTER FIVE

Regional Series and Event Racing

NASCAR has a feeder series. A feeder is a device that gives food to plants or animals. A feeder in NASCAR's case means that these series feed racers to the larger series.

Feeder series are local and regional. Racers start at a local level, do well, and then move into a regional level. From the regional level, they can join the national series with more confidence and skills. Racers who do well in local and regional racing attract national attention and sponsorship. NASCAR has local races covered through the Whelen Series. Regional racing is covered through the Grand National Division.

Whelen Series

A short track is an oval racetrack that is less than 1 mile (1.6 km) long. These tracks are either dirt (packed) or paved. There are many short tracks in the United States and Canada. NASCAR oversees races at 49 of them.

The Whelen All-American Series awards yearly championships to racers at the track, state, and national level. Whelen Engineering

Pictured here is car #31, driven by Steve Park. He is doing a practice lap at the Gateway International Raceway in Illinois for the Busch Silver Celebration 250.

sponsors the series. Each year, more than 10,000 racers compete on local tracks in NASCAR events. The cars are similar to those in the big series, but they are typically not as high end, or costly.

Each driver earns as many NASCAR points as he can throughout the season. To be a track champion, a racer has to earn the most points for that track. State champions will have the most points within a state. The racer with the most points at the end of the season, whether he stayed local or traveled to other NASCAR events, becomes the national champion.

The top three racers in the 2007 national championship standings were Woody Pitkat, Philip Morris (2006 national winner), and Keith

Rocco. Famous racers that began their careers in this racing series include Greg Biffle, Jeff Burton, Dale Earnhardt Jr., Carl Edwards, Bobby Labonte, and Brian Vickers.

Modified and Southern Modified Tours

The Whelen Modified Tour began in 1985. These cars are modified, or changed from their stock origins. They have an open-wheel design, which means that the wheels are not covered by the body. Races

Junior Millers #69 Whelen modified car sits on display in 2005 at the Martinsville Speedway in Virginia.

occur in states including Maine, Massachusetts, Pennsylvania, and New York. Racers that have graduated from the Modified Tour include Geoffrey Bodine, Steve Park, and Jimmy Spencer.

The Southern Modified Tour began in 2005. It uses the same cars as the Modified Tour. It takes place in southeastern U.S. states, such as North Carolina and Virginia. Series graduates include Ralph Brinkley, Ray Hendrick, and Satch Worley. Junior Miller was the first champion in 2005. He won again in 2006.

Grand National Division

The Grand National Division has two series, the Busch East and the Busch West. The Busch East Series takes place on the East Coast. The Busch West Series takes place on the West Coast. Both follow identical rules. The cars are based on those in the Busch Series.

The East Series was formerly known as the Busch North Series. It began in 1987. It takes place in states such as Maine, New Hampshire, Vermont, Connecticut, and New York. Drivers from this series who have gone on to the main series include Martin Truex Jr. and Ricky Craven.

The West Series is the West Coast's oldest stock-car racing series. It began in 1953. It takes place in states such as Oregon, California, Nevada, and Arizona. Big-name racers from this series include Rick Carelli, David Gilliland, Kevin Harvick, Lance Hooper, and Chad Little.

Toyota All-Star Showdown

The Toyota All-Star Showdown is the Daytona 500 of the feeder series. Two thousand seven marked its fifth year. It took place in October at the half-mile (0.8 km) Irwindale Speedway. The Showdown is where

The Toyota All-Star Showdown celebrates racers across the United States. Pictured here are Grand National Division race winner Matt Kobyluck (left) and Tim Schendel, winner of the Elite Division race.

all of the champions come together and race. It is NASCAR's way of allowing leaders, even at the local level, to get attention for the skills they possess.

The first night includes a 150-lap race, featuring super late model racers of the Whelen All-American Series. The actual Showdown involving all of the series' champions is the next day. It is 250 laps, with 40 drivers. The top 15 drivers from the Busch East and West Series are invited to participate. Only the series champions are guaranteed a spot, however. Top drivers must compete in a 50-lap race to earn a spot in the Showdown. Others allowed to participate are the season's champions from the NASCAR Mexico Corona Series and Canadian Tire Series, and all three from the Whelen All-American Series.

Past winners include Austin Cameron, Mike Johnson, David Gilliland, and Matt Kobyluck. Kobyluck told NASCAR, "This was definitely the highlight of my career . . . the best of the best." It is a night where the heart of racing shines. It is also a launching pad for future stars. David Gilliland's win in 2005 made way for his place on Robert Yate's Nextel Cup racing team.

GLOSSARY

appeal likability.

authority Having rule or governing power over something.

avid Dedicated, loyal.

chassis The frame of a car.

controversial Troubled, with debatable issues or concerns.

culture A group of people with a common belief.

dynasty A long line of family power.

hub A center or connecting point.

modified Changed from its original form.

payout Prize or bonus money.

point system A system that keeps track of winnings throughout a season or competition.

purse Prize and bonus monies.

recruit To bring someone into something new.

severe usage kits Kits that were offered to make the suspension of a car stronger.

speedway Major track where automobiles and other vehicles race.

sponsors Individuals or organizations that support another person, organization, or activity by giving money to it.

stock car A car coming from manufactured lines.

suspension The axles, hubs, and spindles of a car, which allow the wheels to connect to the car.

tweak To improve something slightly.

wheelbase The distance from the centerline of the front wheels to the centerline of the rear wheels. A shorter wheelbase allows for quicker turning.

ARCA (Automobile Racing Club of America)
8117 Lewis Avenue
Temperance, MI 48182
(734) 847-6726
Web site: http://www.arcaracing.com
ARCA is a racing series founded in 1953. Many NASCAR racers had
early starts in ARCA.

Canadian Motorsport Hall of Fame
8242 Fifth Line
Halton Hills, ON L7G 4S6
Canada
(905) 876-2454
Web site: http://www.cmhf.ca/index.jsp
This is Canada's leading collection of motorsport historical information.

Motorsports Hall of Fame of America
P.O. Box 194
Novi, MI 48376-0194
(800) 250-RACE (7223)
Web site: http://www.mshf.com/index.htm
This is a collection of historical racing information about Indy cars,
stock cars, Can Am, TransAm, sprint cars, powerboats, truck racing,
drag racing, and motorcycles.

NASA (National Auto Sport Association)
National Office
P.O. Box 21555

Richmond CA 94520

(510) 232-NASA (6272)

Web site: http://www.nasaproracing.com

NASA was formed in 1991 to "deliver high-quality motorsports events to enthusiasts at major racing venues throughout America."

NASCAR (National Association for Stock Car Auto Racing)

1801 West International Speedway Boulevard

Daytona Beach, FL 32114

(386) 253-0611

Web site: http://www.nascar.com

NASCAR is a governing body over national and international stock car series.

Web Sites

Due to the changing nature of Internet links, Rosen Publishing has developed an online list of Web sites related to the subject of this book. This site is updated regularly. Please use this link to access the list:

http://www.rosenlinks.com/hnr/bira

Buckley, James. *Eyewitness NASCAR*. New York, NY: DK Publishing, 2005.

Gigliotti, Jim, and K. C. Kelley. *NASCAR: Authorized Handbook: All You Need to Know*. New York, NY: Reader's Digest Association, 2004.

Mattern, Joanne. *Behind Every Great Driver: Stock Car Teams*. New York, NY: Scholastic Library Publishing, 2006.

Schaefer, A. R., and Betty L. Carlan. *Racing with the Pit Crew* (NASCAR Racing Series). Mankato, MN: Coughlan Publishing, 2005.

Sutton, Richard, and Elizabeth Baquedano. *Car* (Eyewitness Books Series). New York, NY: DK Publishing, 2005.

Walter Foster Publishing. *NASCAR: Learn to Draw Race Cars*. Beverly, MA: Quayside Pub Group, 2006.

Woods, Bob. *NASCAR: The Greatest Races*. New York, NY: Reader's Digest Children's Publishing, 2004.

Woods, Bob. *NASCAR Pit Pass: Behind the Scenes of NASCAR*. New York, NY: Reader's Digest Children's Publishing, 2005.

BIBLIOGRAPHY

Canfield, Jack, Mark V. Hansen, Jeff Aubrey, and Matthew Adams. *Chicken Soup for the NASCAR Soul: Stories of Courage, Speed and Overcoming Adversity*. Deerfield Beach, FL: Health Communications, 2002.

Daytona International Speedway Press Release. "Top Five Greatest Finishes in Daytona 500 History." 2007. Retrieved August 1, 2007 (http://www.daytona500.com/content-display.cfm/cat/Press-Releases/article/6AF9C356-1422-1230-75B42EC51D855303).

Funding Universe. "National Association for Stock Car Auto Racing." 2007. Retrieved August 1, 2007 (http://www.fundinguniverse.com/company-histories/National-Association-for-Stock-Car-Auto-Racing-Company-History.html).

McCormick, Steve. "What Is NASCAR?" About.com. 2007. Retrieved August 1, 2007 (http://nascar.about.com/od/nascar101/f/whatisnascar.htm).

MSNBC. "Harvick Denies Martin First Daytona 500 Win." February 19, 2007. Retrieved August 1, 2007 (http://www.msnbc.msn.com/id/17217075).

MSNBC. "Wild Last Lap Crash Raises Questions." February 18, 2007. Retrieved August 1, 2007 (http://www.msnbc.msn.com/id/17221464/).

NASCAR. *Official NASCAR Trivia: The Ultimate Challenge for NASCAR Fans*. New York, NY: HarperCollins Publishers, 1998.

Woody, Larry. *Along for the Ride: A Collection of Stories from the Fast and Furious World of NASCAR*. Champaign, IL: Sports Publishing LLC, 2003.

INDEX

About the Author

As a child, Holly Cefrey went on weekly trips with her family to the dirt and paved tracks of the Midwest, where her brother, Ethan, raced karts and stock cars. Elaine and Richard, their parents, served as the pit crew. Cefrey's brother raced in World Karting Association (WKA) series and events, including the World Nationals, which take place at Daytona International Speedway. Cefrey was thrilled to be among the pit crew for the races at Daytona. Although she has never raced competitively, Cefrey has taken a few practice laps, thanks to her brother.

Photo Credits

Cover © Jamie Squire/Getty Images; pp. 4–5, p. 12 (bottom) © Jamie Squire/Getty Images; p. 7 © John Harrelson/Getty Images; pp. 10, 16, 22 © Rusty Jarrett/Getty Images; pp. 12 (top), 17 © Bettmann/Corbis; p. © 18 Chief Photographer's Mate Edward G. Martens/U.S. Navy; pp. 20, 25 © David Taylor/Getty Images; p. 26 © Darrell Ingham/ Getty Images; p. 28 © Streeter Lecka/Getty Images; p. 31 © Jonathan Ferrey/ Getty Images; p. 32 © Worth Canoy/Icon SMI; pp. 33, 37 © Robert Laberge/Getty Images; p. 38 © Grant Halverson/Getty Images; p. 40 © Donald Miralle/Getty Images for NASCAR.

Designer: Nelson Sá; **Editor:** Nicholas Croce
Photo Researcher: Amy Feinberg